Going to the Well

Also by Alice Taylor

Memoirs
To School Through the Fields
Quench the Lamp
The Village
Country Days
The Night Before Christmas

Fiction
The Woman of the House

Poetry
The Way We Are
Close to the Earth

Diary
An Irish Country Diary

Children's
The Secrets of the Oak

Alice Taylor
Going to the Well

MOUNT EAGLE

Dedication

To Tade

First published in 1998 by
Mount Eagle Publications Ltd,
Dingle, Co. Kerry, Ireland

ISBN 1 902011 02 3
(original paperback)

10   9   8   7   6   5   4   3   2   1

Typesetting: Red Barn Publishing, Skeagh, Skibbereen, Co. Cork
Cover illustration: detail from "Woman in Farmyard" by Gordon Wetmore,
published in *Ireland Portrayed by Gordon Wetmore* (Thomas Nelson, 1980)
Cover design: Public Communications Centre, Dublin
Printed by ColourBooks Ltd, Dublin

Contents

Countrywoman

Two buckets balanced you
As you drew feed to farm animals;
Hands a map of ravines and ridges
Reflected your farm.
You bought land and held boundaries
Against grabbing neighbours.
Each night you knelt to say your prayers
To a god who demanded as much of you
As you did of yourself.

Revenge

Your sin was dark,
Unforgivable and unforgettable,
But you crawled out of the cesspit
And painfully picked away your filth.
You must have hoped
That your sin would be forgiven.

But we have not forgotten
And now we come for healing
With your destruction in mind.
When you are destroyed
Will we feel better?

Terrible Tidy

The old stone wall
Wore a saddle of ivy.
A screaming strimmer
Stripped it bare.
A demented robin circled
Her shredded home and babies.

Marley Goslings

Yellow yolk goslings
Spattered dewy grass
With webbed feet.
Unwieldy little bundles
Of whipped butter
Slid into the pool,
Golden thistle-down
On brown water.

The Parting Touch

They came to dull your grief
With their kindness:
Big-hearted horsey men
With black forelocks
Over wise eyes.
They stood with you
And shared your hospitality,
Their sorrow not needing articulation.
They were there to ease
Her going from you,
Their presence an ointment
On your wound.

Early next morning
You sat by her
The last silent hour
In the quiet church.
As you left
You placed your hand lightly
On her varnished coffin.

Joe

"Your job is to pray me to my end.
Now I'm not afraid,
That's as it should be.
Ask the Little Flower.
She always saw me through
The sticky bits of my life.
I need her with me now."

So we prayed her final journey,
Her easing from the earth.
She smiled and joked
And was herself.
Her Little Flower
Was there for her
And poured the petals down.

Mother

Awake half the night
Soothing teenage tears of growth,
Listening to splintered emotions.
In another room
A sullen non-talker,
Head buried in pillow.
Come morning:
"Why did you listen to me
Last night?"
From the other:
"Where were you
When I wanted to talk last night?"

Mother's place is in the wrong.

Let Go

For fear of losing,
Held everything tight,
Strangled the very air.
Then quietly let go,
And freedom descended
Like a gentle cloak.

Trust

The dark wave approached,
Sending vibrations of fear
Shuddering up my legs,
Holding me transfixed
In its pathway.
When it crashed down
I lost my footing
And held out helpless hands.
An unknown hand held mine.

When the wave had passed
I was bruised but still standing.

Paper

A glorious thought
To capture on paper!
Hand into pocket
But the pad was gone.
For years it had
Been my companion;
What thief had I allowed
To steal it away?

Well-Being

Your shroud of negativity
Cloaks my thoughts,
Clips my wings,
Pegs me down.
But I will break free
To walk on sunlit hills,
Dance by soothing rivers,
Fly with soaring birds.
Move away from me so that
I can see God again.

Flying High

Flushed in the glow
Of their first red rosettes,
Two little girls sit
On the bedroom floor
And weave golden dreams
Of owning a pony
Jumping at the RDS.
Pony posters ride high
On the walls above,
The sky is the limit:
A world of anticipation
Unfettered by the
Boundaries of reality.

Mary's Ointment

"No flowers or cards.
Donations to famine relief,"
The funeral notice said.
But the old neighbour
Never read the paper,
So he plucked two roses
From his wild bush,
Tied them tightly
With foxy binder twine
And laid them on her coffin.

Mary's sweet-smelling ointment
On the feet of Jesus.

No

Too many strident voices
Disturb the inner well,
Drain off calm waters.
There comes a time,
A time to distance,
A time for no.

Monsters

They slide into our home
Out through the TV screen.
They sit in the midst of us
And we become of no consequence
To ourselves.

Maurice

Long lean body
Supported and borne
On rigid iron sticks.
You have within
A glowing spirituality
In a deep well of words
That overflows and blinds us
To your limitations,
Infusing warmth
Into us who are without
Your buried fire.

Foxglove

Your fingers were never seduced
By the purple petal of a fairy thimble.
Your god walked the streets of man's design.
But you found your way from that crowded
   place
Into the peaceful world of his own creation.
He walks out here along grass-skirted paths
Beneath drooping, honey-scented woodbine,
Singing through birds and running water.
Dew of his laughter on morning clover,
Sun streaks his face in the evening sky.

Going With The Tide

It would have been easy
To turn back then.
Just my toe was in the tide,
Before the warm water washed
Soothingly around my ankles
I could still have broken free.
Instead I went in deeper
And the incoming tide
Crept up along my body
Until I was neck deep
And could no longer turn back.

Excess Baggage

You hung your baggage around my neck
And told me not to feel the weight.
It brought me to my knees.
Painfully I eased you out of my mind
And struggled to my feet.
Then you shifted the weight back
While telling me not to carry
Extra baggage.

But one day the fog lifted
And in a ray of enlightenment
I threw you and your baggage
Out of my mind.

Love

Because you believed
I would light up your life,
I did.
Because you believed
I could do anything,
I did.

Because you think
I am filled with love,
I am.
Because you think
I am beautiful,
I am.

Because you know
I will walk on water,
I will.
Because you know
I will reach for the stars,
I will.

Love enabled me
To do the undoable,
To reach the unreachable,
To attain the unattainable.

It was the combination
That unlocked the vault
Hidden within.

Praying Place

You are always there in a quiet room
Waiting for me to come to you.
This morning, in a hilly field,
Sitting on a mossy ditch,
Listening to the water
Tumbling down the hill
Into the silent river;
Watching the crows fly to work
Across the summer sky,
The rabbits bobbing in the rushes.
Hearing the birds,
Loving the sunshine,
Why was I surprised
To find you there?

Teach me to leave space in my mind
So that you can be always there.

Cow Dung

As a child my feet felt
The three stages of cow dung.
First, warm green slop oozed up
Between pressing toes,
Poulticed sinking heels.
Later sap fermented
Beneath a black crust,
Resisted a probing toe.
Then hard grey patch
Dehydrated and rough
Beneath tender soles,
Its moisture absorbed
Into growing fields.

Noble cow dung fed the earth
Which gave us our daily bread.

High Tide

How did it happen?
Was it the low music and heady wine
That swept us in a rising tide
Of passion into the hotel bedroom?

In the cool of the morning after
The tide had gone out,
Leaving on the bedroom floor
A wrack of discarded underwear.

Choices

Have you forgotten?
Being ten years old
Needing your mothers arms
To be there for you?
Now you bellow down the phone,
Refusing to change dates,
Ranting about public commitment,
But the public soon forget
And childhood has a long memory.

Dawn Crows

Soft blue curtain
Billowing back,
Pale pink stage
Of early dawn.
Dramatic crows
Swooping on
Circling around
In rising
Performances.

Not Again!

There is always something wrong with you,
Your days an ongoing emergency.
You wallow in the drama of life,
Lurching from crisis to crisis.
You never find the quiet times
And all your performances
Demand a captive audience.

But we are growing weary
And are no longer impressed
With your theatrics.

Editor

Wading daily through
Unpruned forests
Of woody words,
Paring the corns
Of would-be writers,
Don't get buried
In discarded hills
Of brain droppings
Lest some day
I come back
And find you
In the waste bin,
Digging, searching,
Looking for
The lost you.

The Key

I have woven
A web of deceit
To protect me,
An adult who cannot read.
I live
In a tangled
Prison of words.
Escape
Is a sentence,
Please help me
To learn.

Christmas in Upton

On this special night
In this holy place,
Where years of praying
Have sanctified the stones,
Let us rejoice
Because we are guests
At the Lord's own table.
He gives to each of us
A heart to love and be loved,
The key to a peaceful
And holy Christmas.

Trapped

Young lambs in a sunlit field,
Too many for the green grass
Where powerful rams dominate,
They jump across the stream
Into wider pastures.
Amongst the larger flocks
They grow tougher coats,
The soft green meadows
Of their youth beckon them,
But they graze further afield
Where the tall grasses bind
And they cannot return.

High-Rise Flowers

Vibrant pink and red
Rooftop garden
In a concrete sea,
Flowers thriving
In grey smoke.
An act of love
Growing quietly
Above thundering traffic.

Old Dresser

Slowly, tediously,
Dead layers of paint
Are scraped away,
A technicolour
Combination
Of many coats.
Then rebirth,
As pale skin
Of the original
Breaks through.
A wondrous moment
When she stands naked
In her pine perfection.

Inner Ice

Life has never thawed
That coldness deep within you,
A lump of ice formed in childhood.
What terrible experience
Quenched your inner light?
Is there warmth beneath
That frozen territory?
Could love soak through
Down into your hidden vault
And melt that icicle of hurt?

Regrowth

Father and daughter
Laugh and argue;
He opens the gate
Of his world for her
But she walks alone.
She has some of the love
That once was mine
And I am glad
That like a garden
We have flowered
Into a new growth.

Wandering Walk

Evening of haze
Laden with summer smells.
Yellow woodbine across
A clustered hedge.
I lift its draping fragrance,
To find beneath the tangled veins
And latticed leaves
Fluttering baby birds
In a mossy dome-shaped nest.

I carry home
Through the warm blue night
The soft swish of silken wings
And the smell of God's earth.

Rejuvenation

Swirls of steam shroud the tired body
Of an old, old woman.
I crawl feebly over the bath edge
And submerge into the sudsy warmth.
My children are parasites,
My husband unloving,
My friends demanding;
I want to die.
My body dissolves,
My mind evaporates,
I become nothing,
Drifting into oblivion.

A few hot water top-ups
And an hour later
I come back together.
My children are independent,
My husband adoring,
My friends supportive.
It's good to be alive
And I high-step
Out of the bath
Vibrant and beautiful,
And the old lady
With all her problems
Disappears down
The plug hole.

Half-Doors

Her arms resting on the half-door,
My grandmother watched the ducks
Swim lazily in the summer pool
While the cows ambled past for milking.
Then, no longer working the land,
She watched calmly across her half-door.

A world and generations later,
In a restored stone house
On a humpy village street,
A sharp-brained literary editor
From busy city streets
With no deep roots in old soil,
Leans on a slatted door,
And yet he now belongs
Behind a half-door.

Train Trees

Gaunt, stark and beautiful
Black ballerinas
On a windswept stage.
We watch you
From a transient train
Dancing on the horizon
For a passing crowd.

Changing Faces

You hide behind the mask
Of a carefree laughing boy
With an unlived in face.
But you are an old old woman
Whose vulnerable heart has bled too much,
Whose sensitive eyes have seen too much.
You hide it behind your mask
Though once it slipped and there
For a fleeting moment was the real face
Tracked by the joys and sorrows of life.

Kindred Spirit

Your fine mind
Uncushioned by the dullness
That makes life bearable,
Penetrated masks,
Heard the unspoken,
Saw the unseen.
On gifted wings
Your artistic imagery
Suffered and sought
Perfection beyond our horizons.

The AGM of the IPPA

We debated motions, rescinded decisions,
Until confused minds voted for and against the
    same issue.
Inflexible, truculent matrons
Created complications, frothed at the mouth,
Tore their sisters' nerves to shreds
To simplify the education of
Pre-school freedom-loving children.

People in Need

"And is three million enough?"
The little girl with troubled eyes
Asked her mother.
"Three million is a lot of money,"
Her mother evasively answered.
"But is it enough?"
The little one persisted.
"No, it is not enough,
But at least it is a mighty effort
To block the rushing river of need
Before it overflows into a black pool of
    despair."

No Switch Off

Are we a passive audience
For the black-faced box
That soaks up life
And pours it forth
On our nightly screens
Where it flows over us
Like soothing custard
On bland plum puddings?

From Different Trees

Beneath the soft green
Sheltering leaves
A pair of doves
Coo in deep-throated
Sensuous love-making.
Close but yet apart,
The warm air
Is filled with the
Heady essence of their
Complete absorption
In each other.

Running

I did not know
It was a race
But I ran
With all the others
Past quiet corners
Where I could have
Picked the daisies,
Past many people
I could have loved.
But there was no time
For it was a race
And the prize at the end
Was death.

Old Jugs

My room is full of old jugs,
Rose patterned, stone and lustre.
And in them are folded letters,
A soft baby shoe,
Key of a house where once I lived.
They are the urns of my life
And I will go to sleep
Here in my attic room
Surrounded by my old jugs.

Tom

Sensitive picture poet,
In your clear vision
Crows fly high,
Rows of little houses
With secret windows
Smile hidden dreams.
Yours is the free
Uncluttered world
Of a mystic child.
Magic trees grow
In fairy places,
In your mind:
The unspoilt world
Of God's creation.

Mountain Face

A great voluptuous woman
Curved in the ample proportions
Of free-range mountains.
Time has carved its furrows
In streams of joy and sadness
Down the hillside of her face.
She bore and reared children
Who went to other lands.
Had she shared great passion
With her hill-farming man?
That she alone will ever know
As her secrets are buried deep.
Her face, like her mountains,
Tells the story of times past
That we can try to read
But she will never tell.

A Scratching Pole

Cows eased
Their arched backs
And unreachable places
On rough-hewn poles
In hilly fields.
A simple thing
That brought comfort
To dumb animals.

Now the poles are gone.
Do the cows no longer
Need to scratch their backs?

The Right Face

He had the inner glow
Of the Risen Christ,
Calm compassionate eyes
In a pale Benedictine face.
His warm reassuring look
Eased unspoken problems,
His face a divine bonus
For his special job.

Reared To It

She was red haired and full of laughter:
"I foster their children when they cannot cope.
My father brought home strays, tramps and
    misfits;
We found them by the fire in the morning,
Crumpled and curled up like toppled-over
    bags of turf.
They were part of his life
And now they are part of mine."

A Lame Duck

He came home
With a duck under his arm.
"She was on the road,
Terrified by fast traffic."
That night I had planned a warm bath,
But the duck swam happily
In my half-filled tub.

Tay

At the door
Two ragged cold wet tinker children:
"Come in, come in."
I made them two cups
Of hot creamy chocolate.
Tentative taste,
A brown stream
Hit the floor.
"Jasus, Missus,
You trying to shagging
Poison us!"
They had never tasted
Its warm chocolate sweetness.
"What would you like?"
"Tay Missus, but let me make it."
She made it in a cup
Black as tar;
She gulped it down
Without milk.
A child-woman
Hardened from the road:
"You can't even make tay,"
She told me,
Her voice filled with disgust.

Help

Even you asked for your chalice to pass,
So do not ask me to bear this cross alone.
The wood weighs heavy on my drooping
    shoulders,
Your crown of thorns pierces deep into my
    brain
And in my stomach the painful gash where
    they lanced.

Because you loved me then you carried the
    cross;
Because you love me now help me to carry
    mine.

In a Small Field

Two cows
Exchanging neck massage,
Exuding contentment:
Bovine bliss on a summer's day.

A Portrait

From behind the easel
Swish of paint on palette,
Scratch of brush on canvas,
Striving stillness,
Sighing endeavour,
Sensuous squeals
Of an artist making love in oils.

Summer Morning

A distant dog breaks the silence of the fields;
Water in a deep glaise plays music
Through rattling brown stones.
The smell of wild woodbine,
Purple clover and whitethorn
Blend the herbal essence of sun-bleached hay.
A crowing pheasant penetrates
The drowsy call of a cooing pigeon,
A multitude of movements
Teems through a living ditch.
Sitting here in the warmth of this summer
    meadow
It is all mine,
The gift of God's real world.

The Other Side

Legs askew,
Cup of tea held high,
Muttering incoherently,
She walks the corridors,
Eyes absent.
We see a lost being
Netted for her safety.
What does she see
When she looks at us?

Transplanted People

After years behind grey walls
They were brought
Into sunlit gardens
But could not run free.
Mental barriers
Held them prisoners,
They were frightened
By our freedom
And wanted home.

Skylight

Long attic room
Hidden high under
The roof of an old hotel.
Liquid moonlight through
A sloping gable window.
We came back there
Late on a summer's night
After a poetry reading
In the orangery
Of a gracious mansion.
I counted the stars,
Smiled at the moon,
Remembering poetry and love.

Stored Summer

Bridal hedges of whitethorn
Cascade on to green fields;
Under bulging wings
The gliding bees
Collect their nectar,
Bearing it back
To humming hives.

Extraction time,
The pregnant combs
Release their ripened treasure,
Pouring golden liquid
Into sparkling jars.

In a deep cupboard
Spirit of warm days
Brings to barren winter
The taste of whitethorn honey.

Forgotten People

Some had blinds
Drawn over eyes
In lonely lost faces.
Other minds peeped out,
Then retreated quickly
Into foggy areas
That sheltered broken thoughts.
Many were blanketed in depression,
All in some way splintered
From the pegs that hold
The everyday together,
They have slipped down
Into the crevices of our world.
They are our forgotten people.

Emigrants

We will come home
When the children are older;
We will come home
When they finish school;
We will come home when they settle.

But the time is never right
And the dream is for ever
Just beyond their finger tips.

The Young and The Old

Long-legged exuberant grandson
Lifts her easily into her pillowed bed
Laughing merrily at her complaints.
Casting aside her sadness,
She smiles fondly at his happy ways.
She had changed his napkins
And filled his childish days with love.
The roles are reversed
And how she needs him now.

Bonded

She is old and tired.
He a strong man of the land,
Smelling of cows and open fields.
He raises her gently with hands
That have lifted a new-born calf
And placed it beneath its mother's head
For her to lick away the film of birth.
Now he rests his frail mother
On her final bed where death
Will lick away the mantle of life.

The Long Night

It is morning.
The grey dawn seeps in,
The fire whispers,
The clock ticks.
My mother's aged face on the pillow
Is tranquil now.
She is weary of long days and nights
Of monotonous inactivity,
Waiting for deliverance
On the welcome wings of death.
But they waft past
And she sighs,
"It is not easy to die!"

The Waiting Window

A warm haze wraps the sleeping hills.
Cows crunch the dew-moist grass.
Birds drift lazily under the skirts
Of billowing trees.
A pheasant stalks the sheltering growth.
White butterflies wing the hedges.
Inside the open window edged with ivy
An old lady sleeps in a cushioned chair.

Fading

Rambling words of a mind
Frayed by years of living.
Flashes of days long past,
Back to the present again,
A record set in repeat grooves,
Wandering thoughts and
Sliding scenes of fading pictures.

Another World

I gathered a bunch of sunshine
To bring into her sick-room
Where days were long and grey.
But she was gone down
A long dark corridor
Leaving behind the brightness
Of our world.

What does she see
As she goes from us,
Feeling her way
Into a distant place?

The Waiting

Death hid behind her chair
But we left her
And stole out into a moist green wood
Where pine and hazel filled the air
With wild freedom.
Long grass fell across our feet
In strands of trailing cobwebs.
We needed that day
Of filtering sun
And laughing birds
To light up the nights
While we waited for death
To emerge from behind her chair.

The Wall

Six rows deep they stood at the wall:
Men with flowing beards and fur hats,
Mysterious men in long black satin coats.
Apart from their beautiful women
With olive skins and raven hair, they prayed;
Elegant and dignified they swayed
Backwards and forwards,
Hands pressed against their wall,
With closed eyes and intense faces.

Jesus, are you with them in their wall?
We believe you are in our host.
You are all things to all people.
They believe you are yet to come.
We believe you came.
But before either of us thought anything
You were.

Why Here, Lord?

Why did you come to this arid land,
Sun-bleached and sun-soaked,
Where camels grind their teeth
And volcanic tempers can sizzle
Into an eruption of violence?

Did you never consider
Coming as a Kerryman?
Kerry is moist and green
And they have many donkeys.
Mary could have ridden one
And made the flight into Cork
From your Kingdom in Kerry.

Perhaps they expected you in Kerry
When they christened it the Kingdom.

Gate of Dung

The gates of Jerusalem,
Ancient walls and sacred places:
My mind stretched to absorb it all.
One golden evening,
My head saturated to overflowing
With holy and historic facts,
A friend and I leaned over a wall,
Looked into a deep chasm.
Thinking venerable thoughts
About an undiscovered David's tomb,
I mused ponderously:
"What is in those hidden depths?"
My friend, a well-earthed man
Of rural Ireland, replied,
"Hard to say, but it would surely
Make a fine slurry pit."

Bethany

Martha the good housekeeper
Welcomed us into her well-kept home
And made us ready for the table of the Lord,
But Mary with her oils eased open my heart
And led me into my inner sanctum.
She unloosed the fetters of my mind
So that I was free to dance with joy.
Thank you, Martha and Mary:
You brought us closer to your friend.

Temptation Mountain

What brought you to this awful place
Near barren Jericho
Where the devil waited?
I could sense him lurking
In those yalla hills.

Peering up against the sun
At temptation peak,
Your desolation poured down.
A rat ran across my path:
The evil was still there.

The Hiding Jesus

Jesus, Mary and Joseph:
There was no trace of you left in Nazareth.
When you went did you pull up your roots
Or are they buried in concrete and chrome.
The architect who designed your church
Never talked with a carpenter like you, Joseph.

Or were we wrong?
We rushed through your childhood place
Where you had time to be a child,
To pick flowers and listen to birds;
I heard no birds and saw no flowers.
But then I was in a hurry.
Here you rode a slow-moving donkey,
And we tried to turn you into a galloping Jesus.
Did you sit with Joseph
In the carpenter's shop and smile at us?

At first I could not find you in Bethlehem,
You were not in the shepherd's field.
Were you hiding in a white hat
Behind a camera clicking away at us?
In the chapel of St James
You flitted in for a moment.

But you came in the Mass,
Came and sat with us,
Filling the little cave
With a loving peace.

A new awareness of you
Was born in me
Which I will find
In every other Mass.

Invitation at Notre-Dame

"Come dance with me," Jesus smiled.
"I can't; my legs are clung to the earth."
"Lift up your eyes and your hands to me
And I will raise you up.
I play beautiful music
But you do not hear.
My music is the bread of life.
I prepare a banquet for you
Yet you are dying of hunger."

Ein Karem

Elizabeth, your home was a summer morning.
The birds in your flower-filled garden
   welcomed us.
As John talked with love about your cousin
   Mary,
A dove cooed gently outside your door.
The narrow path that Mary had travelled
Faded in the distance over the brown hills.

The Three Virgins

Three wise virgins came to Jerusalem.
The guide warned them to mind their money,
Not to drink the water and to watch the salads,
But he forgot to tell them to mind their
    virginity.

The Agony and the Ecstasy

Ann stands at the foot of the cross
And cries with the crucified Christ.
John stands on the hill-top
And laughs with the risen Lord.
Ann cannot leave the shadow,
And John cannot cry with her.

Peter's Field

You were full of enthusiasm
Laced with human weakness.
But because of your great heart
Jesus made you shepherd of his flock.
When we gathered in your field
On the shore of Galilee
You drew us together under a shady tree
With rocks as seats around a little table.
A warm breeze caressed our faces
And flowers and fruits of your fertile valley
Filled the air with their fragrance.

Then when we were ready
You brought your friend Jesus.
We could feel his presence.

Dawn Over Galilee

Above the hunched mountain
The black veil sky
Slowly turns into a golden cloak,
Pouring down over the shoulders of the
   horizon.
Suddenly a brilliant face edges up,
Rising like the resurrection,
Its golden aurora
Blinding our eyes
Streaming a shimmering path
Across the sea to us.
Are we looking
At the face of God?

Going to the Well

She lifts the bucket
Of clear spring water
From the deep brown well.
Before she rests it
On the flat stone outside
The well has refilled,
Gurgling up from the
Bowels of the earth,
Refreshed by use
Like her own pool
Of creativity.

Floating Talk

He lives in the shallows,
Flapping on the surface.
Into the deep pool
He never penetrates,
Afraid of silence
Or meeting himself.

The Gallant Mrs C

The tide of old age
Bore relentlessly in upon you,
But you kept your eyes on far horizons
And swam gallantly against it.
Not for you the "caoinings"
And self-centredness of the old.
You flew a flag of defiance
Against its frailties.
"Why do you never complain?" I asked.
"My mother once told me" you said,
"Gundrede, never indulge in self-pity:
It destroys yourself
And annihilates people."
It was good advice
And you followed it to the letter.

I never thought of you as old
Because your quicksilver mind
Eroded the reality.
You taught our children old-world manners
And outwitted them in jet-age arguments.
And when you should have been
Settling down in your winter woollies
You went to Russia to see the art galleries.
"Don't ever grow old,' you told me,
And you never did.
You came from one of the oldest tribes of Aran
But to me you were also
One of the last outposts of the British Empire.

Own Wings

My daughter,
Poised for flight
From the top branch
Of your childhood tree,
Eager to test your wings:
Wait until you can fly
Lest you become a passenger
On another's thought
And never know the glory
Of free flight
Or feel the challenge
Of your wings against the wind.

The Nun's Strand

The smooth sea swirls silently,
Lapping with a quiet deep calm
Against the black-faced headland
Which opens a wide mouth
And the soft white waves
Roll with a soothing monotony
Between the giant jaw-bones
Along the yellow sandy tongue
Leaving traces of grey spittle
Around its sharp grinders.

Shawls of Silence

Let me creep down
A brown burrow,
Down into the
Quiet womb of the earth.
Deep down where there
Is only silence.
Down, down,
Where velvet darkness
Clothes the ragged mind
In a shawl of gentle stillness.